PIANO DUET PLAY·ALONG VOLUME 7

CLASSICAL MUSIC

PLAYBACK+
Speed • Pitch • Balance • Loop

To access audio, visit:
www.halleonard.com/mylibrary

Enter Code
6533-6111-0559-3787

ISBN 978-1-4234-2190-0

HAL•LEONARD®

7777 W. BLUEMOUND RD. P.O. BOX 13819 MILWAUKEE, WI 53213

In Australia Contact:
Hal Leonard Australia Pty. Ltd.
4 Lentara Court
Cheltenham, Victoria, 3192 Australia
Email: ausadmin@halleonard.com.au

Visit Hal Leonard Online at
www.halleonard.com

AVE MARIA

SECONDO

By FRANZ SCHUBERT

Slowly, with expression

_pp_ _legato_

With pedal

AVE MARIA

PRIMO

By FRANZ SCHUBERT

Slowly, with expression

SECONDO

SECONDO

SECONDO

CANON IN D

SECONDO

By JOHANN PACHELBEL

CANON IN D

PRIMO

By JOHANN PACHELBEL

Andante

SECONDO

PRIMO

DANCE OF THE SUGAR PLUM FAIRY

from THE NUTCRACKER

SECONDO

By PYOTR IL'YICH TCHAIKOVSKY

DANCE OF THE SUGAR PLUM FAIRY

from THE NUTCRACKER

PRIMO

By PYOTR IL'YICH TCHAIKOVSKY

Moderately, in 2

SECONDO

PRIMO

SECONDO

PRIMO

SECONDO

PRIMO

"FINGAL'S CAVE" OVERTURE
(THE HEBRIDES)
SECONDO

By FELIX MENDELSSOHN

Moderately fast

"FINGAL'S CAVE" OVERTURE
(THE HEBRIDES)
PRIMO

By FELIX MENDELSSOHN

Moderately fast

PRIMO

FUNERAL MARCH OF A MARIONETTE

SECONDO

By CHARLES GOUNOD

Allegretto

The Procession

FUNERAL MARCH OF A MARIONETTE

PRIMO

By CHARLES GOUNOD

Allegretto

The Procession

HUMORESQUE

SECONDO

By ANTONÍN DVOŘÁK

HUMORESQUE

PRIMO

By ANTONÍN DVOŘÁK

Moderately

JESU, JOY OF MAN'S DESIRING

SECONDO

By JOHANN SEBASTIAN BACH

JESU, JOY OF MAN'S DESIRING

PRIMO

By JOHANN SEBASTIAN BACH

SECONDO

PRIMO

SECONDO

SECONDO

PRIMO

PIANO CONCERTO NO. 21 IN C MAJOR

("Elvira Madigan")
Second Movement Excerpt

SECONDO

By WOLFGANG AMADEUS MOZART

PIANO CONCERTO NO. 21 IN C MAJOR

("Elvira Madigan")
Second Movement Excerpt

PRIMO

By WOLFGANG AMADEUS MOZART

PRIMO

THE SLEEPING BEAUTY WALTZ

SECONDO

By PYOTR IL'YICH TCHAIKOVSKY

THE SLEEPING BEAUTY WALTZ

PRIMO

By PYOTR IL'YICH TCHAIKOVSKY

Waltz tempo

Valse lente

SECONDO

PRIMO

SECONDO

PRIMO

SECONDO

D.S. al Coda

SECONDO

PIANO FOR TWO
A Variety of Piano Duets from Hal Leonard

ADELE FOR PIANO DUET
Intermediate Level

Eight of Adele's biggest hits arranged especially for intermediate piano duet! Featuring: Chasing Pavements • Hello • Make You Feel My Love • Rolling in the Deep • Set Fire to the Rain • Skyfall • Someone Like You • When We Were Young.
00172162 1 Piano, 4 Hands................................$14.99

THE BEATLES FOR PIANO DUET
Intermediate Level
arr. Eric Baumgartner

Eight great Beatles' songs arranged for piano duet! Titles: Blackbird • Come Together • In My Life • Lucy in the Sky with Diamonds • Michelle • Ob-la-di, Ob-la-da • While My Guitar Gently Weeps • Yellow Submarine.
00275877 1 Piano, 4 Hands $14.99

THE BIG BOOK OF PIANO DUETS

24 great piano duet arrangements! Includes: Beauty and the Beast • Clocks • Edelweiss • Georgia on My Mind • He's a Pirate • Let It Go • Linus and Lucy • Moon River • Yellow Submarine • You are the Sunshine of My Life • and more!
00232851 1 Piano, 4 Hands..............................$17.99

CONTEMPORARY DISNEY DUETS
Intermediate Level

8 great Disney duets: Evermore (from Beauty and the Beast) • How Does a Moment Last Forever (from Beauty and the Beast) • How Far I'll Go (from Moana) • Lava • Let It Go (from Frozen) • Proud Corazon (from Coco) • Remember Me (from Coco) • You're Welcome (from Moana).
00285562 1 Piano, 4 Hands.............................$12.99

EASY CLASSICAL DUETS
Book/Online Audio
Willis Music

7 great piano duets to perform at a recital, play-for-fun, or sightread: By the Beautiful Blue Danube (Strauss) • Eine kleine Nachtmusik (Mozart) • Hungarian Rhapsody No. 5 (Liszt) • Morning from Peer Gynt (Grieg) • Rondeau (Mouret) • Sleeping Beauty Waltz (Tchaikovsky) • Surprise Symphony (Haydn). Includes online audio tracks for the primo and secondo part for download or streaming.
00145767 1 Piano, 4 Hands $12.99

FAVORITE DISNEY SONGS FOR PIANO DUET
Early Intermediate Level

8 great Disney songs creatively arranged for piano duet: Can You Feel the Love Tonight • Do You Want to Build a Snowman • A Dream Is a Wish Your Heart Makes • Supercalifragilisticexpialidocious • That's How You Know • When Will My Life Begin? • You'll Be in My Heart • You've Got a Friend in Me.
00285563 1 Piano, 4 Hands.............................$14.99

FIRST 50 PIANO DUETS YOU SHOULD PLAY

Includes: Autumn Leaves • Bridge over Troubled Water • Chopsticks • Fields of Gold • Hallelujah • Imagine • Lean on Me • Theme from "New York, New York" • Over the Rainbow • Peaceful Easy Feeling • Singin' in the Rain • A Thousand Years • What the World Needs Now Is Love • You Raise Me Up • and more.
00276571 1 Piano, 4 Hands $19.99

GOSPEL DUETS
The Phillip Keveren Series

Eight inspiring hymns arranged by Phillip Keveren for one piano, four hands, including: Church in the Wildwood • His Eye Is on the Sparrow • In the Garden • Just a Closer Walk with Thee • The Old Rugged Cross • Shall We Gather at the River? • There Is Power in the Blood • When the Roll Is Called up Yonder.
00295099 1 Piano, 4 Hands $12.99

THE GREATEST SHOWMAN
by Benj Pasek & Justin Paul
Intermediate Level

Creative piano duet arrangements for the songs: Come Alive • From Now On • The Greatest Show • A Million Dreams • Never Enough • The Other Side • Rewrite the Stars • This Is Me • Tightrope.
00295078 1 Piano, 4 Hands.............................$16.99

BILLY JOEL FOR PIANO DUET
Intermediate Level

8 of the Piano Man's greatest hits – perfect as recital encores, or just for fun! Titles: It's Still Rock and Roll to Me • Just the Way You Are • The Longest Time • My Life • New York State of Mind • Piano Man • She's Always a Woman • Uptown Girl.
00141139 1 Piano, 4 Hands $14.99

HEART AND SOUL & OTHER DUET FAVORITES

8 fun duets arranged for two people playing on one piano. Includes: Any Dream Will Do • Chopsticks • Heart and Soul • Music! Music! Music! (Put Another Nickel In) • On Top of Spaghetti • Raiders March • The Rainbow Connection • Y.M.C.A..
00290541 1 Piano, 4 Hands $12.99

RHAPSODY IN BLUE
George Gershwin/ arr. Brent Edstrom

Originally written for piano and jazz band, "Rhapsody in Blue" was later orchestrated by Ferde Grofe. This intimate adaptation for piano duet delivers access to advancing pianists and provides an exciting musical collaboration and adventure!
00125150 1 Piano, 4 Hands $14.99

RIVER FLOWS IN YOU & OTHER SONGS FOR PIANO DUET
Intermediate Level

10 great songs including the title song and: All of Me (Piano Guys) • Bella's Lullaby • Beyond • Chariots of Fire • Dawn • Forrest Gump - Main Title (Feather Theme) • Primavera • Somewhere in Time • Watermark.
00141055 1 Piano, 4 Hands $12.99

TOP HITS FOR EASY PIANO DUET
Book/Online Audio
arr. David Pearl

10 great songs with backing tracks: Despacito (Justin Bieber ft. Luis Fonsi & Daddy Yankee) • Havana (Camila Cabello ft. Young Thug • High Hopes (Panic! At the Disco) • A Million Dreams (*The Greatest Showman*) • Perfect (Ed Sheeran) • Senorita (Camila Cabello & Shawn Mendes) • Shallow (Lady Gaga & Bradley Cooper) • Someone You Loved (Lewis Capaldi) • Speechless (*Aladdin*) • Sucker (Jonas Brothers).
00326133 1 Piano, 4 Hands.............................$12.99

HAL•LEONARD®
www.halleonard.com